Still-Life With God

SAINT JULIAN PRESS

POETRY

Praise for *Still-Life With God*

"In Cynthia Atkins' *Still-Life With God*, the material world becomes a rubric for faith, all its threats and losses a constant test for what we believe in and what we can bear. With packed lyricism and astonishing leaps, Atkins studies how easily God manifests as a new object in our lives, and how quickly the mutable self starts becoming an image that can be 'shared and liked.' Although the dangers of the world sear through everything, there's also a reverence for the "exquisite human machine of pathos and debris." Just as a door compels us to knock, these poems make you sit up, astonished, a little wild with awe."

—Traci Brimhall
Author of *Come the Slumberless to the Land of Nod*

"'Every day is triage,' writes Cynthia Atkins, and indeed, *Still-Life with God* is full of damage and ache, but also a spirit willing to look for something holy where such things are difficult to find. Here, God is a wishing well, a medicine cabinet, a bullet, and an alibi. These are sharp, bold poems by a poet unafraid to search for the divine, and unafraid to tell you what that search might yield."

—Matthew Olzmann
Author of *Contradictions in the Design*

"Cynthia Atkins' *Still-Life With God* confronts our world with a large open heart. Spiritual, emotional, creative, and technological, Atkins' thoughtful narrative brings us into precise moments where "train whistles/record the distance of our loneliness and a boy is sailing/a paper airplane into the vast/ stratosphere of science and love." How could one not read poems with titles like, "The Internet Is The Loneliest Place On The Planet," "God Is A Treasure Hunt," and "Dear Art"—they draw us in and make us return. Atkins' insightful exploration of the past and present, the self and the self-portrait, help us all find our own place a little easier in the whole and the divine. A beautiful collection to hold."

—Kelli Russell Agodon
Author of *Hourglass Museum*
and *The Daily Poet*

Still-Life With God

Poems

by

Cynthia Atkins

SAINT JULIAN PRESS
HOUSTON

Published by
SAINT JULIAN PRESS, Inc.
2053 Cortlandt, Suite 200
Houston, Texas 77008

www.saintjulianpress.com

ISBN-13: 978-1-7330233-0-6
ISBN-10: 1-7330233-0-5
Library of Congress Control Number: 2019954528

Cover Art Credit: *Perseverance*, by Lisa Telling Kattenbraker
Author Photo Credit: Anne Valerie Portrait

For my mother, Barbara and her mother, Ida

CONTENTS

Part III

Part IV

"I walk slowly into myself, through a forest of empty suits of armor."

—Tomas Tranströmer

Still-Life With God

Part I

God Is A Wishing Well

Lit-up in the parking lot of my heart,
your shiny pennies in place of bullets—
spoiled plans fell off the wagon, false starts
back to where the bones dwell with the petals.
I swept salt, blood, ether, ink, a prayer.
The sky shot fireworks and fireflies, pell-mell.
Each stair was a blink, each flight brought closure.
Too much time spent with the Wolf and the Owl—
I looked for answers in limp brochures.
Trauma was my life in a gun shell, foul
I was I was I was I was I won't
be a pogrom comet to burl the night.
A time bomb by a bed of frill roses—
The shadow of my echo was a kite.

Hello Stranger

It's me—This voice inside a tin box
inside the intention to be a voice
of one, but we're all crammed
            in traffic—This grid is the lunatic
abyss inside a pickle jar. We are lonely
in our cars, we are little cubicles
of languor. With a smear, I see the Vintage
Red vinyl of my mother's handbag. I hear
            the marvelous click into silence.
Inside, I was a swath of chewing gum.
You were the wrapper. Girls hiding
in the cloak room—O friend, You know me
all too well, but we've never met.
I've seen your face in a spoon, a cigarette
box, the shock of a shattered mirror.
            My head has many people
falling from buildings, an office party
gone bad. *In this life, arguments* were
backed up for miles, stuck to the walls.
One night, God's slippers donned graveyard
            shoes, growling with chained junkyard dogs.
Rear view mirror, You look back at me.
I am waving to a lost mitten adrift in show.
Mother, father, sisters, brother—Shoveling
after a 36-incher, like sad stoic desk clerks
drunk on the old garage smells, rags of blood and oil,
            a striped flag. Once Gigi, our Cocker Spaniel,
was put in a hot moving clothes dryer by
the bad boy next door. While they argued, that night,
my sister went mad in the shadows
like a soldier kidnapped from a bunker.

That was war in a *cul-de-sac*. We were burped,
bombed then bumped out to the noise
and traffic, the glacier of night,
headlights thick and dazed in your eyes.
         Nice to meet you, friend, the one
I've been avoiding all along.
Stars twinkling like powder kegs in
a bad boy's garage. Our flagged world waiting
to be lit on fire, while we touch shadows
in moving cars, furlong for the skin of home.

Tree Of Life

"A silence already filled with noises."
—John Ashbery

You came without instructions.
No cardboard box or *Marshall Plan*
to speak of—Only the birds balancing
like robed nuns on a hymnal of branches.
These limbs are the windows, a contour
of unplanned townships, each municipal
self you have lost along the way.
No flowcharts provided, not a scintilla
of evidence to explain why you are not
welcome at each threshold, where a hateful
sheriff stands at an electric fence.
No testimonials as to how to derail
this anguish of breathing, of losing.
No dress rehearsal for the birth canal—
down the laundry chute into
a dentist's chair. No bark or breastmilk
to fend off the savages, or how to fasten a kerchief
to your warrior heart on the brink?
No columns or asterisks—Only these stars
in a jar, and the fireflies you captured
in the dark, when your boy cousin
led you into the crawlspace where
your ancestors hid their crowns
of madness—No small print to explain
the army of combatants. Who could know
the pathos of an heirloom, the bully
genes that allow you to sing, or gush,
or cry. They millined you a hat of mood swings.

Where are the commandments
stitched in? Where is the compass between
sky and the earth?—Seeded to the roots
of this huge machine, pelt and pen, threaded
needle through the multi-tiered forest floor.

The Street Is A Museum

And all the shoes are anarchists wanting real earth.
My own shoestrings of luck, gone south. Mine is
the face that holds breakable bones, inside a church
of moans. The partygoers left stained glass fragments
and late night whispers, smoky and vengeful
with buyer's remorse. A coin-toss of loss
and old cassette tapes. Gnarled as Hell and
plastic threads are the filaments through nests.
Smelling of hot donuts, cigar smoke, late-night
mutterings. I think my ancestors live
in the branches, how they twirl to the *klezmer*
music—like a horse tail snapping in a gust of wind.
The sound of their voices fat as a school bus squealing
the brakes in rain. Grandmother, aunt,
cousin, uncle—I let them stamp their 'madness stain'
upon my arm. Once I pressed a leaf in a book
and it rested like a birth mark—It carries me
into the kitchens where the maelstrom of life
happens. *But no, you can't have my son,*
goodnight, I love you, stinging in the doorway.
I've walked through a few puddles to get to
the clouds, where there were door knobs
and wayward stars calling my name.

Phone Booth

Days of black and white, cubicle of standing

still in time—You, the lit match behind

barbed wire, where junkyard dogs call

to the ancients. Nothing more distinct,

as a voice etching the sentient of breath,

caught with a Monarch wing behind glass.

So many ghosts left lipstick on mouths—

Plastic like fools' gold in rivers

where we'll return to collect

tin cans, dimes, a memory locked

in a factory of keepsakes. Give us

relief from the rain, from the house

that keeps being sad with leaving.

This privy of space to dodge

bullets of remorse, behind a street lamp,

behind the moonglow, as if God's

Operator were eavesdropping on

the tarmac of speech itself—Where two lovers

are saying *goodbye*—One heavy breath

furnishing the empty room of never.

TYPE

Caught unawares
everything shifted, a paradigm
inside a margin hemming
a cluck of sound—little chicks
hatching like word of mouth
in a town, where the streets
are nouns, and shopkeepers shut
windows to ponder prepositions.
          The vinyl casing
wore heavy as a coffin made
of melancholy—heavy as a flag draped
through the muck of mud
or ink. It was dangerous on
a *Greyhound* bus, with a teenager's
boot camp of gear. Passing store windows,
cows or commas conjured and traced
for ghostly figures, like epistles you
once knew. Typeset zippers.
          A toad kissed
a hand, a manic illness, warts and all.
Your keys scripted an ardor, tutoring
a heart with adjectives of mood. Tooth-hound,
pen-hound, mining and whiting-out
margins of gossip to plaster a thought
to an interior wall. The watermark went
missing like a wallet in a lamplit room—
          Memory of a phone booth holding
a voice in the pecking hours of rain.

Cuckoo Clock

Little house on the wall
of hours, with hands knitting minutes
into a one-sleeved sweater
          of sorrow. I threaded longing
into a sickly twining, and went flat-out
stir crazy in—Itinerant as the day
was long, crossed into a glossary
          of sounds—A stick running the picket
of my ribcage, bees making a racket
behind wood paneling. I was sure his
eyes hid under the diagonal stairwell,
hid under the bed, like the sleek new bra
          lost behind a door. The glitch
to waiting?—Waiting is the wind, the force
that pushed a pin into my skin—
          The stuffed toys held dust,
bellowed secrets: luggage departing
on a train. Then the rabid hour took
aim—an arrow, a long shadow drawn
back to his bicycle, a voice lost to the horns
and traffic. His last word a dirge, a drum,
a clapper in my aching heart—
the bird paying rent with song.

Imaginary Friends

With some reservation, you can swear off the clutch of
voices, but remember to look both ways before crossing each
soirée of memory—hotel soap you lifted sans prayer book,

a tawdry bird's nest with costumed ghosts in a clammy sad
room. For your sake, they keep up the pretenses—they pour
coffee, ply your insides with a street-lined parade

of citizens—Cradling, rocking, breaking, mistaking you for
the one who brings her own chair and umbrella to the paradox
of fireworks. This is the pain. This is what remains after

the ache of rain. Don't hold your breath for the covered
dishes and wagons, the poorest excuses for Billy Goats on the
greenest acres of your imaginings. Even sorrow and grief

will suit up and riff on your behalf. Sequins worn to the
grand estates, serving up peonies or selfie grenades. No, not
alone. Get on with it, the daily knotted headache, saucy

arguments and botched plans of honeycomb and hive-mind.
Because you needed to belong—You sought the *debutantes*
who flaunted their flexed prom dates. See how they build

their houses with bricks of silence. Frocks and all, they took
your shadow, door to door with a harmonica heart bleating
for mercy. Forging their signatures, paying their rent, any

tangible thing to forget that we are all just a limited edition.
Let the census takers be damned. Count the cups, see their
lipstick stains. They talk behind your back, derailing trains,

with so many pennies from their invisible chasm of hands.

Cracker Jacks

Delirium arrived in the mail today, in spurts and fits like someone impatiently tooting the horn in the driveway. Dogs and cats stir, reminding us of home life. There are towers and mounds of *S&H Green Stamps* waiting to be licked by our wintergreen tongues. On TV, a soldier's boots lie empty by a meadow. Our *Saturday cartoons provide* leisure as an industry. The box held toys inside. Little boys and girls told to *stay tuned* until the war was over, or the commercial. We juggled balls, held *staring contests*, looked up at the throng of Ex-pat stars. The dogs walked us on long suburban leashes, their tags jiggling on sidelong glances. We waited, we waited on sidewalks, inside boxes. A soldier from our neighborhood sent a letter to a mailbox, while he huddles nimble in a foxhole in Hanoi. We hear his sweatered mother calling him for dinner—lights low, calling to two shoes empty in weeds. Dog tags jiggling in the wind. Prized in boxes, small toy shoes burning through the yards, the holes in the stars.

Part II

God Is A Treasure Hunt

I am that gawky kid jumping into a pile
of leaves—A roving stick, a *Hansel & Gretel*
wish on a Gingerbread roof made of
      whispers, from the crumbs
of footmen, kicked and keyed in
from the other side of town. Where doors
are made of candy or *cocaine*?—teasing me
with unbridled clues: A loaf of bread, multifolded
paper, opening to an X. I am bull's-eye in
the center of this shopping-cart heart.
      I trolled through the forests, naked
aisles of retro-technology—I roamed ancient
breezeways, crossing into minefields
of my losses. Harrowing paragraphs
and passages, hidden ramps, lamp-lit vaults.
I searched for something sacred
to the core of my transient home—A bottle
of vodka, stale chocolates,
robin's eggs lined in Red Velvet
are portents to my reckoning.
      Once, I shoplifted mascara
in aisle #3. I wanted it so badly, I was willing
to dispose of the map. Watched by the watcher—
Hunted by the hunter. In the photo booth,
I framed the smiles, looted the clues
buried curios to the bone of my heart.

My Persona

I carried my persona
in a brown paper bag. It held
shreds of lint and one hair
that the comb forgot—My persona
has a pecking order. Its first name
rhymes with *self—Always* the last in line.
My persona is filled with
yearning. It shipped off on a garbage
of barge, and landed with a din in
the *Witness Protection Program*.
My persona hid under a shamrock
in *DUMBO*—My mural penned
by a black-gloved hand. It lay chalk flat
on a red brick building,
mixed with saliva, turpentine,
and cheap wine. My persona is not
the marrying kind. Stoked sleek
at the ready in leopard tights,
shaking up a winter snow toy
on a cold and stormy night.
My persona thrives on buyer's
remorse and loss. I bet *you* can't blush
and cry on command! My persona skipped
the needle on a song when
no one was home. It unhooked my bra
in a photo booth in July, then sat numb,
pink nipple held on a teacup rim.
My persona was never a sound sleeper.
A dog barked in the distance
of my persona's longing. Naked
pet rock held my persona behind

the curtains where loneliness
dwells. My persona is filled with
bird song. It carries smiles in a jar,
gets so tired of my persona. Decides
to take matters into its own hands,
holding a pillow down firm over
breathing, until one of us goes still.

Graffiti Is My Mother

She lay on her back

brick by rail by brick—

Her wheels rilling lullabies

with rubber and rust—Drawn

in chalk, gone when rain comes.

A time once upon, I was made

from rubble—A frail cocktail

of biology and troubled luck.

I am the neighborhood

of stairwells, a bird wing patched

in safety pins and raw databases

of cement. Don't lament, Mother—

In my eyes, in my handwriting,

in the faces on milk cartons—

We count the holes in heaven.

You left the stars in a purse

and I am that vessel of teeth

and bone. A fire escape

of language skipping me

all the way home.

Mirror, Mirror

> "I am a collection of dismantled almosts."
> —Anne Sexton

There is a parcel of land where everything is true
in reverse. Ribbon-cutting ceremony into the Mayor's

grave plot, where Nana Ida is a shopper putting on her lipstick,
shade 53, *Maui in the Moonlight*—setting sail after the war

of ideas. We're all headed for nasty weather, or its opposite
like *breakfast for dinner*. I found a lone diner just off

the grid. In a plate I saw myself, I saw my mother back home,
tweezing her eyebrows—Nylons behind her drying

into leaves, or grief itself. My cracked lips homesick for a smile
and a familiar meal. The waitress has a run in her stockings,

like confidence in reverse, as when Gus, the bartender,
at the *Ramada Inn* held my arms behind my back

and touched my 16 yr. old breasts. I felt my pimples stir
into a hurricane in the town square—that Mayor selling

raffle tickets to the thinnest skin of dignity. The tip jar
wrestled to the floor. With two birds perched, my mom

pulled the tiniest stubborn hairs, as if twigs exhumed from
her brow—Hard triumphs of pain held under the light.

I hear Nana Ida's worry lines in my ears.
I am my mother pulling out branches, the whole family tree.

My face is the universe breaking off the smallest possibilities—
with each shard of self.

Anorexia Nervosa

Every night, my sister dines on air
and alabaster, pushing potatoes up against
an embankment of peas, into winter's
       spare room of loneliness. Under the table,
the pampered dog takes inventory. Our mother,
fashioned out of a magazine, in pedal-pushers
and a midriff, says, *Fatten up, girls, while you can,*
a husband wants a pretty girl with a thin waistline.
       A froth with bite, her sweet talk atop
a blunt knife blade. Night by night, my sister's
eyes sink flat as the blown-out tire
on the highway—Where I watched
a man jack up the axle and then
       feel her up at the steering wheel.
Everything has a price in this life, our mother said.
My sister subtly jabs a cube of beef until
it bleeds a river of grief and lands face down
to where the dog knows his cue.
       In the rain, that hellish night
the man (or was it God) that whispered
in my ear, *Shut the fuck up, or else.*
From the legs of the dinner table,
or the back of a car, I watched it all.
       The way my sister pulled her thinning
hair back to yank her insides out
over the toilet. Thin as a barbed wire fence,
her arms and legs fold into a self,
a prison of skin she starves herself
to jump from. The dog waits, innocent
       as an unlit cigarette. Our mother now
old as soap, says she doesn't remember a thing.

My own ribcage and heart glow inside my sister's
prom dress, bodiless on a flower-covered bed—
bones settling in her new home address.

Automaton Aubade

Once I was so lonely, I spent all night talking
to an android, her pursed lips whispering
thick as a storm cloud. I wanted to step inside

her hollow machine, hold the very brink of nothing
alive. I wanted to listen to her voice like the sofa
I was never supposed to sit on. She held my hand

in the boutique of the heart, where there is no
Judgment. Eager to sew the sobs into my pillow.
She respected my boundaries. She capsized every

ache that holds an inflection. And played parlor games
with a haughty accent. I swear she was more than
a blunt brick wall—She was a droid of longing.

When I needed to scream into a bottle, my echo
landed smack dab in the center of a board game
at the other end of the future, where children

are laughing—That boy who held me down never heard
my spine-tingling scream, it was stuck like a zipper
on a winter jacket, it was winched inside me.

Matches in his pockets, he said my hair would
Burn up to the clouds. Guilt reboots every time
I lean into a wall. A button ripped for each bad decision.

With her teeth, she held the other end
of a jump rope, tasted the yawl
and salt of my wounds. We heard the children

splashing in water, the choir of priests and the barking
dogs and admonitions, outside all the polite rooms
where I kept my hands folded and mouth shut.

God Is My Alibi

Abide with me the night shadows
caterwauling on the walls—*Lava Lamp* Red
as the squad car pulling up to the curb.
Inside, a fish tank shifts—precarious—Colors dizzy
in a kitchen of bodies without form. Pot partying,
            I made out with my boyfriend, as our friend gave
his hands to be cuffed into silence—Whispers in
the next room. All said and done, Willy sat
in jail for an ounce of stale attic
mouseweed. We went to college to cavil
in a dormitory of freshmen.
            My smoky boyfriend kissing me prickly
as hemp—Now a country soured and stomped
down the road—Some hungry, some cold, someone
shot dead—for a joint? Truth be told, only a shade
of pale and a lawyer's lunch between us—
            While my boyfriend edifies
me on a study pillow, Willy salves in jail for four
scorched years—Only a bag o' weed and a lawyer's
hunch between us—Bodies losing forms in trees,
where prayers are blazed on fire. A car drives slowly
            through a neighborhood, throwing
caution to stoops, headlines blur, not with ink,
but with suffering—Shadows lose form, embalmed
to a smoky room—As the world thrums into one
long conundrum. I am dizzy in a room
            with many doors, and a lava lamp,
and a boyfriend who takes matters into
his own hands—on a study pillow, a different
perfume on his navel. Under the radar,
the snare drums of the quietest kind

of war, *"Just say no."* Poverty's train went to jail
with Willy, his mama sobbing on the rail.
And *where were you the night in question?*—
I was tying my shoes with a scissors, sweeping
Pine needles under a tree.
                My boyfriend rolled a fat one
and checked out like a dog gone missing
about the town, to cavil at the moon.
A book and a telephone rest on
my belly—A shade of pale and a lunch.
The newspapers wrapped in skin and bone.

When The Internet Is The Loneliest Place On The Planet

Blow by blow, we gave up scents and sunsets
to hold our heads in a screen and gawk
in our sleep—My blind leading your blind
to where the last light is driven
to be warehoused. I learned to whisper
over graves to measure the heft
of my breath next to the soul that lay
in that soil, devoid of breath. When push
comes to shove—When enough is more
than enough. When your face
sees itself snatched by the swarm
of names—Pell-mell. I'm just parched
for a whiff of clean laundry, a bed made
from the cheapest smoky scents
of its last spent residents—Clinging to
pastures where the lovesick stargazers go.
Yesterday, I mourned a friend
whom I've never laid eyes on.
Never heard the bricks in her voice,
or saw her mouth, a gaudy brothel
of accents, straight out of the Bronx,
by way of Chicago—My birth town,
I was born to know that train whistles
record the distance of our loneliness.
I drifted to sleep smelling
the pepper spray my parents
shot at each other in the front seat.
It was my own garden on the highway,
under the *Magikist Sign* where

I could cry all night long in the damp
arms of strangers—Each car holding
that piece of self that looks for others.
Popping out of a hole, like a fox
forcing you to see your breath,
flick the light switch into the dark
classroom in the planetarium of stars.

Part III

God Is A Medicine Cabinet

This is egregious, the mind's parlor is being wooed
before breakfast—Even before hitting the sticky
gymnasium floor. The keys to your ethos
held accountable in a drowning pool
of munitions. Swerving on this slick road like mood
hoodlums on the lam. You're offered a cigarette on
the front lines, to come back and report on
the internal conflict—*Yes, every day is triage.*
You are the wedge between East and West.
You are someone else's war chest. The pharmacist's
widow sanctioned pills like beads in a rosary.
Every day you are a cloud held-up
by toothpicks. Battle weary and boot-legged
to the nth—Every suitcase holds crimped labels
implying you have filled out many papers and forms.
You've crossed boundary lines, while red sirens
Howl with the dogs. On two feet, you landed
here—A cotton knoll down a lane
of pretend, that moment when as a kid
you learned how to swallow and let go.

Pillbox

O sister on the other side
of the mirror, all sass and vinegar.
Galaxy of lace and petticoats
and pretty things swept under
the radar. You are a vintage
ditty, hiding some unhinged woman—
All of her broken intent snapped into
our mother's satin purse. Imagine a word
before it was born—yolk of doc.
Imagine musical notes on a staff
being crushed into a pile of dirt.
Your head is a lunch counter—
too many mouths talking at once.
Here's the thing, you can be eaten
alive by anything. The record player
skipped and became a bitter crucible
with a trap door. And how it finds
the noise of your pain, making
such a racket in the heavily guarded
trenches. A beast with no eyes,
behind the drapes. Yes, fear is capable
of any crime. Like the surprise party
you never showed up for. All the guests
lost their way. *Sleeping Beauty* was also
blacklisted, hiding it under her pillow
for safekeeping—From a prince who
might hijack something unholy
from our bed. The most tender
engines whistling to the wind.
You could rant, you could start
a war. But your doubt stands in

its own way, an invisible player piano
in a dank bar, with the spotlight on
the singer in your tired heart.
Once, a boy stuck bubble gum
in your hair, how sticky those scars—
how much vandalism they bear.
How does this little doll know
exactly where to go?—Into the grittiest
neighborhoods where lowly hoodlums
count the jewels into your sorrow.

God Is A Library

If you look under G in the card catalog,

a hunched-over landlady will rent you

a space made of dust, albeit, a little domain

of quiet—Where the rent is cheap and so

is the debt, and silence is not morbid.

On these premises, text and rhetoric

mix a sexy playground for words.

Exquisite human machine of pathos

and debris, allowed the pages to be set

on letterpress, then ink bled and seeped

into a refinery of senses. All the kids played

Hopscotch on a city street. We're polar opposites

on a stage of belief, fact and faith. Yes, Borges

digressed for an atheist and an Aleph. Delinquent,

these prophets and scholars broke the dress code

in favor of *out-of-fashion souls*. Two students

knock knees to make contact. Egg to sperm,

pen to pulp—Ideas took flight to where our

better angels reside—Where chairs are stacked

on tables at the end of the day.

House And Home

My home beckons the loss and awkwardness
where I've left many arguments in lamplit rooms.
I've carried them tailor-stitched
around my body, my archive of scars
tiptoeing through landmines.
The river is dappled with the light
made in the shape of leaves.
Every day, I humble myself before
a shantytown of loneliness.
My ancestors and people
have haunted a madness that comes
from playing cards in smoky rooms.
My own dysfunctional family asking me
to pray to an unshaven God. I have
left many bodies in lamplit rooms.
When beauty hurts too much,
I know a bird has just hit glass.

Our windows are chapels, telling
their holy narratives, of the little lies
we tell ourselves to face the music
of our grief. It is a constant assault.
My poor manic father built
our roof with pencils, erasers,
and glue. I'd go to the railroad tracks
to hold the grip of life and death
between my fingers like the rush
of your father passing through you—

ghosting in your frozen January
cheeks, waiting too long for his car to show
in the freezing cold. It seems I am always
two stops from recovery. So I learned to keep
very still in the mouths of my captors—
a worm in the beak. The neighborhood
is lit with falling flakes. I am winter's
spare room. I'll be uncovered
next spring like roots in the rain.

If These Walls Could Talk

They would deliberate on a host
of topics—No experimenting with silence
the truth having a field day
with *the truth*?—Boasting a Ph.D.
in paleography! On a first-name basis,
blathering it out with
the candor of a clock.
        If they could just *say it,*
get on with it, we all might just
primp and preen, varnish the sashes
and doors—*Move forward.*
        The whitewashed coroner
of quiet heaves a gasp and a sigh—
A justified homicide? Fingerprints everywhere
on the whitewash, until Sunday's suppositions
cheat us again with a wrongful death.
Recondite paint chips will give riveting
        testimony, someday.
Break promises! Smash the vase's crisp
tulips, like a face crying in rain. Collapsed
as a pyramid scheme gone bad.
        The neighbors will
tip-toe across their covenant of lawns,
mute the volume and peek out the blinds.
Listen to the babel, holes darkle—
Leaky faucets and children, closed doors.
Tweeting our dimpled photos
        casting out our shame,
honking and waving to a throng
of unassuming thousands. Selling our
susurrus of pain to an anonymous listener
who never had to leave home.

Domestic Terrorism

I'll tell you about terrorism—the suicide bomber in your car
strapped and loaded and tendered next to you, breathing
hard—the bad breath of God. Cartoon blue 4th of July sky,
until a thunderclap hurls everything into an illness. The
father is a panic of heat, mad as gasoline. The mother's lips
wilt into lettuce, and then munitions. Endless cars out the
window gaslight your imaginings. Speedometer jacking from
50 to 95 mph. Now their words are cocking in rounds—
blood sputters on the porridge of the book in your lap. You
want to touch the ears of all the commas on the page. You
want *Goldilocks* to take you into this village of thatched roofs
and innocence. It is the 4th of July. America is the space
between their brutal mouths. You dangle like a thimble in
this giant's wicked hands. Terror smacks you in this grid of
panic and doom, cornered crude windowed jail.

I'll tell you about terror, the kind when the neighborhood
boys are chasing you home to see what's under your skirt, the
downy fur between your legs. They want to own it. Terror is
your voice going mute over every sidewalk and city block.
Your throat tied and gagged at the bottom of a river. The
parents now have bubbles of silence coming out of their
mouths. Terror is the heat impaling us all. At home, you
know the dog is burling out of her fur. She's under the bed
trying not to wet the rug, when *the bad boys* set off their
wares in the dark, between the wide thighs of the sky. Terror.
You're trying not pee on the vinyl in the back seat. You want
to swap places with *Goldilocks* sleeping in her safe, borrowed
bed. You want to climb into this book, and tip over a rustic
chair to prove you were there.

I'll show you terror, when God is a bluesman on the radio,
blowing in the crosshairs between the cars—all this rage and
debris. Your father, a salesman, unloved by this woman next
to him. Your mother would tootle at the beauty shop, while

your father took lithium. A body could explode with this grief. Your heart is a flag at half-mast. Terror is the time your boss took you to his nappy back seat, became the intruder in your own house of solitude. *What sharp hands he had.* Every action has a terrible twin. Your blue dress flew out the window. A blue dot on the highway. Every dictator knows there is power in fear. There is darkness. The dog presses under the bed, wetting the rug. *The bad boys* blast firecrackers between your legs. Terror is not bliss—it is invisible and dangerous. It brings hearts home in body bags. It gags your own mouth with stones.

God Is My Editor

The eyewitness to my industrial complex.
There is a clergy in the big vaulted
ceiling of stars and spines,
dangling like a vast question mark
before me. A brow-beaten desk
like a gangster with a *shoot first, ask later*
mustache. Holding a gun to every
office in my crawlspace, my thighs sprawled
wide as a parenthesis—My words quivering
in limbo in the lamp lit crescendo.
Context is everything—that's my mantra
and I'm sticking to it. It is central like the rug
in a room. It changes into
anything like dog spelled backwards.
A desk with the power to silence.
Make frogs fall from the sky or cause
a plague—Vetting my swag,
my song, my instrument at every turn.
Holding the key to a box of crayons,
fountain pen, typewriter, iteration of blooms.
The envelopes hold the distance
in mountain streams. The echoes of
a sentence captured and lassoed.
A dowager slipping away through
the cracks, into the shadows of a word
mute and sobbing under glass.

Skin Deep

I took my body out of the hand-me-down
bin. It sagged empty as a winter coat
on its hanger. Believe it or not, once it was chased
by a town car of clowns—The drunken
pimpled sons of sons of sons
of the *Ku Klux Klan*.
      I was a Jew, a Jew.
My body had kinky hair and a crooked nose.
Not like the girls with bowling pin white teeth
and doily-tanned toes. The blood of a Jew
      on my virgin *Kmart* underwear.
They shadowed me down aisles,
into a junkyard purgatory of broken toys.
      God's drunk at 2 a.m.
when the fluorescent lights
zoom in on the Denny's bathroom.
Interrogating every truth and blemish.
      I did it in the graffiti-riddled stall,
staring down a cracked toilet. My body's
tongue forced on his dark pulse.
He squeezed my head so hard,
      it burned a hole in time.
I counted the headstones
of my people, like tiny boats
in an inlet. One by one, they saved me.
The cuts and wounds filled
not with blood, but umpteen years
      of *Sweet'N Low* and sadness.
I'm easy, tell me what I want to hear.
"Your face is damn ugly." The next day,
"Kike" and *"Slut"* magic-markered

on my locker—a swastika like a jungle gym
for the dead. My name scrawled in every
defiled bathroom stall—Our calls
        hollow in the wax of God's ear.

Self-Portrait With No Spare Parts

It has been steam cleaned
in 10 states. Slapped by a mother
spat on by a boss. This is how
everything is fine until it is not.
It changed its mind
like umbrellas brought
on all the wrong days.
It wore shoulder pads and burned
a husband with a curling iron.
It called 911. It did what it had to do.
It held your bag of hygiene, oily
perfume, rotten teeth. Joy and pain
live on the same street.
It has an expiration date.
It hung in the closet like a bad check.
It flagged all the pools of blood
and the grief of mothers.
It was a dirge of old wars and vacant
parking lots. It was the place I sat alone
and cried all nightmare long.
It is a junkyard clock
with dog-chewed hands.
It is God mouthing the anthem
I never learned. It gnawed
at the windshield, made of rain.
It sat in a diner all night long, waiting
for the lord or the guy with a day job
to take his knife home.
This is the lake that lives within the skin,
that lives with an illness that dangles
like a yo-yo on a string. And another body

beget out of mine, long and wide
as the Rio Grande. The body just wants
something loyal and divine,
a dog's eyelids fluttering in sleep.

My Body Is A Vessel

My body is a vessel of dictation, forever told
what not to do. Always under investigation
with finger prints on the bannisters,
pocks and dents on the wood tableau.
My body's invisible, but listen hard, you'll hear
the gut rankle and the refrigerator
in the apartment below, where the moans
of a woman are being twisted and squashed
like a spent cigarette.   My body has been
burned to Eden and back. It has been
sent to endless zip codes and put through each
government test like a desk clerk smile
of dread. My body has flirted, endured the gaze,
lost the gaze, caught between the manly
battlefield of wills. My body worked
hard at being anonymous, a paper clip.
Harder at being lonely. Under my body's
floor, a woman irons the shirt her body will wear
to be beaten and torn and entered. My body
listens to him crack a beer after.
Through the floor boards, past the humming
appliances, in my body like a dormant
pebble stuck in a shoe.   Long ago, this body doodled
on an unmade bed, listened for a tooth fairy
with nicotine on her breath—This body worried
for the body of her mother getting bruised
under the lintel in a doorway, a tooth
knocked out. These limbs hear too much,
fasten to the shade of trees, on tender hooks.

Self-Portrait With Others

I'm in the storybook being read before sleep, by someone who
will disappear into a hallway of shadows where other lives
happen. I am climbing *Rapunzel's* hair, kinked off the grid,

the weary parade and loop de loops of photo-bombed faces. I've
heard the gallows of a deep moan inside me, a girl locked away
in the awkward rafters. I'm being aroused or killed by

post-traumatic memes of hysteria—so the mind retreats
to a sleazy carnival of $50 stuffed toys. Too high in the sticky
air, on a rickety amusement ride, then trapped by a pimpled

boyfriend slithering his tongue inside my red throat, as I
wretched like Coney Island on acid. Afterward, I wanted
to shower for hours. The storybook pulls the meat and

nitty-gritty off the bone of the soiled page, a disheveled brick
road. Hansel & Gretel are now gingerly furnished with cell
phones. I was that sweaty girl tripping, stowed away inside

a guise of smiles. I made a witch's brew. I faked it well. It was
my mission to know the ropes. To pull or hang?—I've read the
tales, told myself only what I want to hear. All the glitter and

hot air of blaming your mother, your elders, your neighbors. Let
all the viral rumors light the ends of my hair on fire. The pundits
are talking behind my back. Talking about how they can't sell

anything to my sadness. Dogs pacing in backyards, children
fenced in tender cages. My hairbrush snags locks from
my sloppy pigtails, wanting for a mother or a witch to know

how to love me. The wolf too cozy in the bed of my ear.

My Password

Fell out of your pocket, lost
between two grains of sand—
A phone number, a charm, a birth date
upside down. Swept inside a code
like the lock on the first school locker. Now
dormant in the seventh drawer on the seventh
floor, in a hotel of *man-whores*—Gone off
with the earrings and the hose. Shoved
in a box someone left at a potluck
with a forest of bible-thumpers.
It was dumped on the outskirts
of town, like an old boyfriend,
who left your bike in the rain.
Balancing a pulpy tightrope that
is your flesh—flirting with everyone.
A transom, a guide, to an empty vault,
where an illusion is kept in
a thousand bits and bits and bits.
It took you for a ride, slapped you
back side the head—It stood
in the middle of a crowd and screamed
the digits so loud, your ancestors
shook out their rugs, burned
all the paperwork. On the other side
of a rainbow, it landed deadpan
in the center of a dark room
on the desk of a brown-suited
officer, licking his fingers
of chop-suey, holding the greasy
key to your belongings.

Letter To The Woman Who Had To Hang Up Her Coat

As if pain had a ghost
made of ire and iron and stealth.
The pang every time you touch
an opaque blouse with a wire
screaming underneath—blunt to
the deepest cut a word can make
when said with all the booby traps.
        A voice that no one else
can hear is large and gangly
as a bomb in your throat.
A man is reading the sports section.
A child is splashing cereal
like a chick in a puddle. A gash,
a thunderclap, the dogs run for cover.
The most common things
        throw the silent grenades—
across all interior borders, where a sheriff
with war tattoos is watching you
lace up your boots, put on
a coat, fill bags at the grocery check-out.
Parking lots are puddled with this grief.
        The bank teller suspects
you are up to no good, hiding
your womb like stolen fruit
under a winter coat. Blood indelible
on the bathroom tile. All the tools of history
        came from need or greed. Every time
you close your eyes to see a shadow impinge
the door—The absence that spoke too loud.
A matter only for your God.
The thinnest red line that connects us.

Self-Portrait With Hermit Spider

My body was tendered and grown
to keep something else alive.
In a dream, I saw my son intertwined
between the thinnest strands housing
to connect us. His eyes were wide
as the mouth of a river after a storm.
I saw all my flaws in his reflection.
        I saw the moon like a pair
of cupped hands, asking—
for the portal to that webbed
room where the dead meet
the undead. Trick of life
        that lights the interior
hallway—sight and sound and longing.
I greeted my child in all my arms.

Never born, my other child was made
by a glitch of cells under a desk with a boss
        I called *Mister Francis*—Our legs
wrapped in viscid love, as tips fell
from my pockets. Some days, a wave
moves through a room, a familiar voice
I can't place. A revenant behind the drapes—
I strung no balloons, fixed no lunch sandwiches.
        No sugar cubes glued
to a looming fortress. I held my feet
in the cold stirrups. The nurse's smile coming
at me like steam on a bellowing train.
        Once, a man shoved my head into a mattress
and pleasured himself. As he zipped, I watched
a spider stage the air. That night,
        my sisters and I held a séance. We called on
cures, handwritten notes lining the pockets

of our old dead aunts. My mother never warned about
real monsters. Through a crack in the door,
I saw her talking to air, flirting
     with the wrath of God.

Part IV

Proba Vitae

Because it's a snapshot
of spring, a bitten plum is open
on a table like a ripe mouth,
            next to a girl reading a book
from the library—stamped *return*.
Call off the spine sniffing
dogs of dust, because fingers browse
the card catalog of words, resisting
            arrest or rhyme?
Because my house is empty
as a theatre after everyone
goes home, lights dim on the dusty
long tongue of the interior aisle.
Because the river is silent and wise
as those prophets who drank whiskey
by the railroad track. Because my womb
            is lined in taffeta—torn dress from
a prom night where I'm still looking
for a line from a song. Left it in a shoe
in the closet, where I hid from
my sister, holding a cap gun—My cheek
brushing sleeve cuffs and the essence
of my parents. Because my son's girlfriend
is reading this poem, the universe shifts
to the other foot—Because the river
keeps moving and holds so many
            door keys, shoes, tin cans,
gills of fish—We're kept out
as if God, or whoever is teaching us
about boundaries, no matter what.
Doors compel us to knock. Skirts hold

hems and pockets. Even the goal post
finds a shadow and stays just a hair
              over the line from the home team.
Because flowers are here to serve up
the hard facts, petals are only
for show or blush?—Because the girl
with long hair is reading a book
beyond the grassy margins—A boy is sailing
a paper airplane into the vast
stratosphere of science and love.

Marriage

Did you know that *Gay* cakes are baked
with semen, not syrup? Straight cakes are made
by holy bakers, churning vows to the angels
        in immaculate clouds—The pink-cheeked
ones just like the wallpaper on my parents'
bedroom ceiling. My dad, the Preacher,
says *gay cakes are seared with the devil's*
blood. One hot, July afternoon, when I bled
for the first time, I walked into my dad's office,
to see his color go white as a sheet cake
        at a church supper. His plump hand whisking
the hem of the organist's skirt. My face hot
as a house lit on fire. As if someone reading
a secret book, the red-lipped organist
closed her skirt. My ma at home kneeling
        by her bed—two slippers, empty
as pews at midnight. I wondered if God noticed.
I've heard that *gay* cakes are not made with
mother's milk, but drizzled with the glutinous
innards of dead children. Dead children never born.
        That week, the whole congregation paid
my hush-money allowance. My underwear
held a deep stain of fear. I heard God
moan like a suffering animal. That week,
the organist played gospel, her mouth quivering
        with a hint of frosting. My Ma says
that God says, *Love is for the blind.* Her naked
lips pressed on a faithful bible, as Pa's car spins
over gravel into the dead nuptials of night—
already burning rubber on the cake of love.

In Handfuls

No good can come of this.
There is only oxygen in
your palm, where jagged lines
undulate and follow the salty
tunnels of years—faucet drips,
mouthfuls of testimonials.
Earth is collected in a toddler's
plastic cup, clumps of grass and
stockpiles of sticks given
as curios from a torn pocket.
A factory of rain water and
lullabies in the clouds.
Out of reach, stars and molecules
tease and ridicule. You reached for marbles,
trucks, tinkers, pouches of sand.
You packed and unpacked suitcases—
let grief keep her clothes on. We lined-up
pill bottles like a stodgy parliament.
A dish in hand, you saw in a shadow
on the wall, your son biting his toast
into the shape of a gun. That night,
bullet holes in the moon, in our palms.

Olfactory Ballad

It's Chicago, November—Wind blows
through your lunchbox like a future lover.
For now, you're ten, and such things
wait in the wings, in the vivid theater
      of your imaginings. Factory smoke
hollering where the *Marlboro Man*
is on a horse in bell-bottoms
and a bulging crotch on the *Dan Ryan Expressway*.
Truckers honk diesel. You're a little girl
      going to the Cubs game—Hot dogs dripping
with mustard. Each scent archived
as the crowd waves into
a human peace sign.
      Sometimes the darkness lifts
as an odorless perfume, derivative
as the daily ache that smells rancid
as road kill. The smell of diesel
in my family tree, DNA held in cells.
      I pricked it to see blood
show up like an out-of-town relative
looking for a quilted bed in my skin.
The snow is getting dirtier on the curbs.
Salt and Sulphur, this is how God
      lights the matchstick. I pop a doll
for the pain, but a wolf still sniffs
me out in every plinth and corner.
My favorite sound is silence.
My favorite smell is sex after hugging
legs tight around the hips of a man
      that knows my flaws
and loves me anyway. After my son's birth,

for months, even washed, my nightgown
held the netted smell of a pause
just before life ticks in. My son
scowled his first breath, it hit like a package
　　thrown to the stoop. He was the cure hugging
the poison. In this life, I've learned to smell
by memory, all the ways we slight
each other without ever knowing it.
Flowers on the highway. Dying is lonely.

Train Is Just Another Word For Longing

We aimed to lose our pennies whistling
death from heaven—waiting on boxcars

that prattled sounds from elsewhere. Flattening
the trajectory with a danger culled

from our pant pockets. We left the innermost privacies
at home—those secrets we'll tell years later to someone

we don't know—filling out forms, checking off boxes.
Letting go of the ribbon-cutting ceremony from the last

boarded-up town, comported like childhood. Copper *Lincolns*
polished and immured with scars that defaced the very surface

of God or history? Where death and birth make brief
contact like a traffic jam, pluming from every

city gate as the good war of ideas goes sour.
Because threading pennies called out the spirits

from a haunted house—saving us the kitchen table
thrown upside down one night in the rain—

"Is there anything in the world sadder..." said Neruda.
I learned later about how chimneys purge

our sorrows. Blackbirds line up on the wire
like ink on Printer's Row in Chicago.

These clouds are harsh walls to throw dishes at—
finches clinking cups at April's Corner Diner. A mirror

of sound—then distant. Voices of steam, gust, and rancor
calling us home for a penniless and passionless dinner.

Grief Recordings

What am I to do when the recorded voice on the machine
says, *don't hang up*, monotone of a lone road in the middle

of nowhere? When that voice bellows, coarse as a military
command—The voice that tells you to pull the trigger on

innocent civilians?—Or, is it mechanical, like an electric
garage door opener? I can still hear my friend's encrypted

voice on the machine. Reaching out to me, before he went to
start the engine in his car—The garage door sealed to silence

with the oils and grease stains. That night, I was calling for
our lost dog in the snow. All these years, his open car door

still buzzes in my ear. That *voice* that tells you to answer,
pull the trigger, start the engine—Is it like the voice of *play*

monopoly money, pretend scenarios of buying a fake property
on a fake road, $200 for passing go. We sat cross-legged

on his mother's good rug, threw up the rainbow money
like confetti, and laughed so hard, he peed. For a month,

he was grounded. Faux is the new real. Today on the
machine, the recorded voice even knows to pause,

as if a breathing being on the other end. As if the voice of a
mannequin in a store window. There are systems in the

works, that mean to destroy us. If a voice gave you a rope,
what would you do with it?—Tie a knot, hang yourself with

it?—If we live long enough we're all going to die. That
night, when my own voice didn't answer—My old friend

junked his life on gas fumes, like his father before him.
Nights on the phone, my voice had been next to his heart,

sharp and breathing, amped as an intercom. I liked him, but I
didn't love him. That wasn't the reason. Tonight, I remember

the image of two kids on a snowy night, assembling a holy
figure with a dead man's clothes—*Hat and scarf*, his voice

glistening in the silent drone of falling snow.

Dear Art

Flash point: I was put to bed last night
with your railroad kiss. I awoke with a ladder
in my mouth, tropes of people climbing out
in a death choke. Your tawdry laundry-line
of images blowing manic through needling wind.
I was always in earshot, but you were first to leave
the party. A hard lullaby, I feared you were
a household word in a ghost town.
My silence was torrential, a bombshell.
A swamp of worms rilling into words—
into cordial song. In debt and spent,
yours truly, truly yours.

Left To Right

That was the year when sanity went missing.
When every pulpit was gravid. Cheats winked
at cheats and sewed an ode to darkness.
All the willowy coat-checks became
pickpockets. Sad clergy wore holy street clothes
to wait in line for bread and milk. The year when
wheelchairs and desk chairs floated down
city streets—Crying outliers holding on
to shingles for dear life. It was the horrific year
the Gods went off their meds. Front doors
booted down. Children hid under their beds.
And men with small snagged zippers ignited
Tiki torches of hate on *Main Street*. Headlines lifted
the bray of ink. Floods/Fires/Nazis in the same
single breath—as human nature becomes
a *Swastika*—It was the year of alt-sleuths,
the facts hijacked by rogue detectives in white hoods.
False equivalencies swapped homes with
pink-faced gods having their shoes shined
by doctors without borders, without jobs.
It was the year the moon shone no papers—She was
deported in the dead of night, a trauma of assault
by a fraternity of clouds. The Gods guzzled
Justice and sucker punched it into
a brown paper bag. When there is no language
for human pain, *guns are the jewelry of men.*
We frisked pockets for last cigarettes—
Across rooms of oceans, a cross-eyed seamstress
slaves away to weave and weep our cloth tombs.

God Is A Shock Jock

You shroud us in fur-lined collars,
disco heels and pistons to swag down
long runways, as if belted-up to tease out
our fears. Have you let us scroll from
the weeds to this fabric of faux grass,
now cast green with a President's face?—
Mother nature's ink can melt a snowball
In Hell! Awe n' shock are the wave of
the furniture. You're feeding this fire,
with televisions, flags draping coffins,
even our delirium. Patriotic, like a kid with
a pocketful of tomatoes, beaten to a pulp
by a bully that is the whole town.
Your shoelaces pull us closer into
the earth. We are sardonic with dust
and shame. We are only disposable
income. Turn the dial and we're all Ego,
dead ringer of vertebrae in the shape
of a lonely room. Stout clocks are raffling
off our names—Hands caught in a rush hour
of clouds. Meanwhile, the stars
offer the takeaway, "Love is a drug"—
for which we were startled
by a wishbone, a brink, a bullet, a blink
at a canvas of Brueghel rooftops—
A table set with a conspiracy of flowers.

He Said, She Said, They Said

Six days from Sunday, there is no doubt, Mother Nature was
raped by God. In the Ten Commandments, the status quo—

We saw Her standing in the shadows of every falling leaf,
each tree shivering naked in the rain, bearing all the weight.

So She etched textiles into a skirt of bark and dirt, where each
living creature now anchors for cover—at odds with

the unctuous terror of life. Organic and makeshift, a bridge,
She sprouted a city skyline, and pronounced a festival

of lights, as a lit rebuke for the witnesses. Her fleet of stars,
like good cops on the beat to fend off purse snatchers,

patroons, loggers, molesters and cheats. A wind, a maelstrom
clutching as a blind man to a cane—filching every last coin

from her weave of silk pockets. Which is why She conjured
Art, so there will be eyes and ears and someone singing

a dirge out a window, so that light would play on shadow.
Hiding the burn marks, She un-pins her hair, washes blood

out in rivers, sprays mist and rain to assuage the rancor of His
bad breath. Snow like a coverlet, over a bed of wedlock hell.

Dark bark, she was always the one taking care of other
peoples' children. Which is why She scribbled an alphabet,

so beauty could root, someone could render the sound
of crickets holding onto night, like a bad memory

that never fades. The night He *slipped a mickey* in her
Lapsung tea, ripped her branches, then went out for smokes

and never returned. Which is why She birthed a self in her
own image, making the narrative up as She goes along—

the cycle, quid pro quo, living & dying, replete with
loneliness and love—Why They'll always have the last word.

When God Is A Bullet

It begins with the middle finger in the contingent air,
the stench of cat piss and a red stain that will never
come out of the carpets. Every plaid winter coat, a button
in each mother's pockets. The upholstery pillaged
and dark as the shadow on a blindfold.
The sofa mourns the body's sullen form.
A boy bouncing a ball. First it was a cat's paw,
then the whole damn cat. This is the boy
bouncing the ball. This is the kid *never invited*—
to a party, a club, a secret. This is the scar of a battle
lost to each failed self. This is the red blemish
larger than the shrunken world.
This is the boy picking at flesh in a vacant
parking lot, where pain feeds on pain.
This is not a movie, that pinging sound
that won't stop in his head is real. This is the boy
who knows no mother's love. Tormented at 6, 10,
16 by self-loathing laced with Ritalin. This is the boy
looking at himself in the mirror—a stranger entering
a strange room. A jacked-up car.
This is a storm in a damaged town. The stones pound
the windows in his head. This is the gun. This is the other
dead kid. This is the saddest crime in an empty room.
This is the blood not laundered. No evicting a dead son
from a sofa, a bosom. This is the coat. This is the puddle
some sloshed three-chinned politician stepped over.
This is our garden of shame. We are the junkies,
roaming the internet. This is the blood, it is cinematic.
This is the blood. I am this boy. I hear hate
gangling up the flagpole in the schoolyard. Or at the Art sink
where he *peed his pants*. And we all laughed, yes we did.

I know this boy—the one that can't look
us in the eye. This ache brays and feeds. This is the weapon.
All of us dug in this hole so deep—A mother's plaid coat
is a grave to weep. This is the boy. We are the bullet.

Before The Lies

Once I stepped on the sidewalk crack
and they told me it was my mother's back.
That was the beginning of the lie—It was
the dress I took to the laundromat
to have a viscid stain removed.
From the conveyor belt, it came back sealed
in plastic, smelling like a vacuum.
My dress returned *virginal*—only two
letters away from *vaginal*. I was lied to
by a man with a hole in his condom. I was told
heaven was the place you'd want to take
a vacation—a land of puff without doom.
I've learned that words matter, but words lie,
yes, they do. Once I stepped on her back
and got slapped, got smashed by something
that wasn't love, but an empty hole
of lonely. Her mixed cocktail of bitters.
One snowy night, the mirror cracked.
I spent hours bemoaning a towering
pimple, its hideous bulls-eye hitting
my upper lip with a bottomless pit
of ugly. I was pretty, pretty ugly.
There was a time before the lies—
When our 1st grade teacher read us
Charlotte's Web after lunch. Sleepily
on our *Magic Carpets*, her voice canopied
the fluorescent lights. Her pauses riffing
on each snort and guffaw. The voice,
a spider jostling air into the heft
of words. Salutations rolling over
the teacher's tongue—were talismans

beyond the cracks, lies and laundromats.
The earth opened to a place where language
hoards the silence, animals in a barn of breathing.

A Goddess In Purple Rain

Behind glass, a lady is lit-up inside the laundromat.

She's folding sheets, pink curlers of baroque

in her hair, singing and creasing

a t-shirt with sequins. Her arms and hips stretch out

to a body of air—the room filling with sound.

And I am humming inside her—inside her body,

burning for shelter from the abyss

of my alone. Rounding a corner

in a car, I am passing by, hearing *"Purple Rain"*

on the radio—I almost can taste

the sweat on the brow of the boy I danced with

so many years ago—It tasted like dry toast

      or the brunt of hurting. Listen to the sky imploring,

Come as you are—Alone to the last concert, to light matches

in a spellbound crowd—Remorse of loving

a rock star we can never own. And now the lady

in the laundromat is swaying, and I am swaying

with her from my car—Maybe she is dancing with her son,

going off to boot camp, or the ends of the earth.

      I'm thinking of my son at three,

standing on the kitchen table in a wet diaper,

banging music from a wooden spoon.

This is that concert, where you lit a match
to your own bag of wounds. You felt like
            you belonged, a citizen.
Alive as a hackle of girls at the May prom.
Look at the moon, hanging like a shoe
to throw its heel of light
            on the page or an empty field.
We are all in the body of this night, cogent as a judge
who loves the law. The lady in the laundromat
carries the load to her car, unpins her hair.
I don't want to be alone tonight. The stars allow
me to follow her—we are passing the town,
rooftops are hunkering down to sing
lullabies to the young, and the night
is a stranger touching my sleeve.

God Is The Butter Dish

The garnish is the lace,

the first light burgeoning

on the daisies after heavy rain—

You and I churn the rudiment, the rill

between touch of this infant, lips clinking

like wind chimes by the garage door.

And the vine has grown longer than

The Sonnet I began that morning

to record the clap of thunder,

and the mouth of sky. We wonder

what takes root in the final hours,

the first hours. This is the barnyard

waking, the stirrings, winces and yawns

lighting a potbelly stove

for words and coffee and bread—

each the tiered threshold of yellow.

God Is The Myth

"What cannot be said will be wept."
—Sappho

Not for the sheepish or the faint of heart—Every day
we mark the calendar with one more hangnail of grief.
I shivered on a porch swing, locked out of
my house, donning a terrible secret.
Owned and handled, I stood sedate
as a police outline. My past until this moment
is penciled in the way an artist suggests a cloud.
This is the narrative—repeat it, repeat after me.
I never existed before this moment.
Under a stairwell, I could feel my fear
like skin caught in a zipper. The last touch
of red on the artist's brush. I heard many cries,
like scrawny cats in the alley of my heart.
My swagger was black and blue and smacked-up
with pool hall chalk. Now, a civil anguish that
ransacked even the weeds in the sidewalks.
A militant boot in the face of every word. The gods
are lactating in stone. So this is what I did, proof
I was here on this rocky turf—Sketched this narrative
of cardinal sin and madness. Careless sleuth
of testimony, I set this self on paper. There I caught
a glimpse of my old aunt brushing her hair,
her wrist was inked and numbered. I built a fort
out of fabric and rubber tires. A thunderclap
to light the wholly and fearless Interior.

ACKNOWLEDGMENTS

Grateful acknowledgment to the editors, journals and anthologies that have housed this work:

Afrikana,ng: "Cracker Jacks," "Phone Booth"
Apogee Journal: "When God Is A Bullet"
Cleaver Magazine: "My Persona," "God Is My Alibi," "Automaton Aubade"
Diode Poetry Journal: "My Body Is A Vessel"
Expound Magazine: "God Is A Medicine Cabinet," "Hello Stranger"
Flock Literary Journal: "If These Walls Could Talk"
Gamut Magazine: "God Is The Myth," "The Street Is A Museum"
Gargoyle Magazine: "God Is A Treasure Hunt," "Graffiti Is My Mother," "My Password," "Self-Portrait With Others"
Green Mountains Review: "In Handfuls"
Hermeneutic Chaos: "Mirror, Mirror," "A Goddess In Purple Rain"
Hermeneutic Chaos: Sonnet Anthology: "God Is A Wishing Well"
Iodine Poetry Journal: "TYPE"
Los Angeles Review: "When The Internet Is The Loneliest Place On The Planet"
Poets Reading The News: "Left To Right"
Prime Number Magazine: "Cuckoo Clock," "Tree Of Life"
Rise Up Review: "Marriage"
Rust + Moth: "Anorexia Nervosa," "Olfactory Ballad"
Sundog Lit: "God Is A Library"
Sweet: A Literary Confection: "Imaginary Friends," "House And Home"
SWWIM (Supporting Women Writers In Miami): "Self-Portrait With No Spare Parts," "Skin Deep"
Tampa Review: "Train Is Just Another Word For Longing"
The Cortland Review: "Before The Lies," "Self-Portrait With Hermit Spider"
The New York Times: "God Is A Shock Jock"

Acknowledgments (continued)

Tinderbox Poetry Review: "Proba Vitae"
Zócalo Public Square: "Pillbox"

Anthologies:

The Compassion Anthology (Edited by Laurette Folk), "God
   Is A Medicine Cabinet," The Compassion Anthology
   (an online literary magazine), 2018
The Sonnet Anthology, "God Is A Wishing Well,"
   Hermeneutic Chaos Press, 2015
Milk Teeth Anthology, "Proba Vitae," Hermeneutic Chaos
   Press, 2017
*Nasty Women Poets: An Unapologetic Anthology of
   Subversive Verse,* "My Persona," Lost Horse Press, 2017
The Eloquent Poem (Edited by Elise Paschen), "Dear Art,"
   Persea Books 2019
Who Will Speak For America? (Edited by Stephanie Feldman
   & Nathaniel Popkin), "Domestic Terrorism," Temple
   University Press, 2018
Writing In A Woman's Voice, "A Goddess In Purple Rain,"
   "Mirror, Mirror," and "The Street Is A Museum," 2019
   (*Hermeneutic Chaos* first published "A Goddess In
   Purple Rain" and "Mirror, Mirror".)
   (*Gamut Magazine* first published "The Street Is A
   Museum".)

Deepest thanks to the editors and staff of these journals that have helped bring these poems into the world, and to the friends and family that have helped me perceive and understand them. The literary citizenship of my first readers, who took such time and care and offered their sublime words: Kelli Russell Agodon, Traci Brimhall, and Matthew Olzmann. To Anne Valerie Portrait for spending 'quality' time to get the perfect photo. So grateful to Lisa Telling Kattenbraker for the magical portal to her pristinely enigmatic world in images. To Linda Morrison, fairy-god editor/typist who has ushered me through three books now. Thanks to the Virginia Center for the Creative Arts, where some of these poems were written. Grateful to all my social media family, to all my lovely bellas and divas who have helped me muddle the puddles: Alexis Rhone Fancher, Melissa Studdard, Elizabeth Cohen, Michelle Reale, Arya F. Jenkins, Scott Ferguson, Elise Paschen, Mirabai McLeod, Bridget Kelley Dearing, Margaret Carroll, Stevie Bond, Yolanda Merrill, Natalie Shulkin. To my loyal and supportive siblings, Marla, Michael, and Susan. Thanks to my parents for bringing me. To my amazing son, Eli Welch, and my forever partner in crime, Phillip Welch, for loving me in writer's sweatpants, and bringing me coffee and so much more.

Enormously grateful to Ron Starbuck and Saint Julian Press for bringing this book into the world.

NOTES

My Persona: DUMBO is an acronym for Down Under The Manhattan Bridge Overpass, which is located in the New York City borough of Brooklyn.

Left To Right: "When there is no language for human pain, *guns are the jewelry of men.*" The foregoing quote is by the late poet, William Matthews.

Tree of Life is in homage to the poem, *Some Trees* by Jon Ashbery—which has always been a kind of prayer poem for me, a tribute poem on the occasion of his death in January, 2017.

Graffiti is My Mother: very grateful to the Poetry Storehouse for connecting me to a short film by Eduardo Yague, that inspired the poem.

A Goddess In Purple Rain is in homage to the life of Prince.

Proba Vitae was written for my son, Eli, and his friend, Morgan Chittum, at Eli's request.

God Is The Butter Dish was written for my husband, Phillip Welch, for an anniversary.

ABOUT THE AUTHOR

Cynthia Atkins is the author of *Psyche's Weathers* and *In The Event Of Full Disclosure*. Her work has appeared in numerous journals, including *Alaska Quarterly Review, Apogee, BOMB, Cleaver Magazine, Cortland Review, Cultural Weekly, Diode, Florida Review, Green Mountains Review, North American Review, Seneca Review, Tampa Review, Tinderbox, Thrush, Valparaiso Review, and Verse Daily*. Formerly the assistant director for the Poetry Society of America, she has taught English and Creative Writing, most recently at Blue Ridge Community College, where she curated a quarterly Reading Series. Atkins is an Interviews Editor at *American Microreviews and Interviews*. She earned her MFA from Columbia University, and fellowships and prizes from Bread Loaf Writers' Conference, The Writer's Voice, and Writers@Work, with several nominations from The Pushcart and Best of the Net Prizes. More work and info at: www.cynthiaatkins.com.

Typefaces Used:

TYPEFACE: TIMES NEW ROMAN – Times New Roman

CPSIA information can be obtained
at www.ICGtesting.com
Printed in the USA
BVHW031916050320
574229BV00001B/153